?" i-8 HAR

37628

Ideas of the Modern World

Democracy

Nathaniel Harris

HODDER
Wayland

an imprint of Hodder Children's Books

Copyright © Hodder Wayland 2001

Published in Great Britain in 2001 by Hodder Wayland, an imprint of Hodder Children's Books.

This book was prepared for Hodder Wayland by Ruth Nason.

Series design: Simon Borrough

The right of Nathaniel Harris to be identified as the author of this work has been asserted by him in accordance with the Copyright, Designs and Patents Act 1988.

A catalogue record for this book is available from the British Library.

ISBN 0 7502 2748 6

Printed and bound in Italy
by G. Canale & C.S.p.a., Turin

Hodder Children's Books
A division of Hodder Headline Limited
338 Euston Road, London NW1 3BH

Acknowledgements
The author and publishers thank the following for permission to reproduce photographs:

AKG, London: pages 11, 15; Bridgeman Art Library: pages 20 (Department of the Environment, London), 22 (Private Collection), 23 (British Museum, London), 33 (British Library, London); Camera Press: page 5r; Capitol Collection, Washington, USA/Bridgeman Art Library: page 25; Giraudon/Bridgeman Art Library: page 30; Hulton Getty: pages 19, 21, 31, 32, 39, 40, 42; Index/Bridgeman Art Library: page 12; Lauros Giraudon/Bridgeman Art Library: page 24; Peter Newark's American Pictures: pages 4, 26, 37; Popperfoto: cover, pages 1, 5l, 6, 9, 17, 35, 36, 41, 43, 45, 46, 47, 48, 49, 50, 51, 52, 53, 54, 57; Roger-Viollet, Paris/Bridgeman Art Library: pages 13, 27, 29.

Picture on page 3: A vote is taken in the European Parliament.

Contents

Democracy 4

The Ancient World 10

Centuries of Change 18

Towards Democracy 31

Ideas in Conflict 40

The Continuing Struggle 47

Issues of Today 54

Date List 60

Glossary 62

Resources 63

Index 64

Democracy

As an idea, democracy is quite straightforward: it means 'rule by the people'. The idea was first clearly expressed by the ancient Greeks, who combined the words *demos* (people) and *krates* (rule) to create a term that is now used all over the world.

In modern times, democracy seems to have triumphed. Most present-day countries either are or pretend to be democracies. Their political systems may differ, but they all claim to be based on a belief in popular sovereignty. (Used in this way, 'popular' does not mean 'widely liked' but 'to do with the people'.) Popular sovereignty is the doctrine that final authority in the state belongs to the people (that is, to the adult members of the community). From this it follows that any power exercised by governments is only legitimate if it is based on the wishes, or at least the consent, of the people. It also follows that, in a democracy, all adults are citizens, that is, individuals with full political rights which they can exercise freely. Political freedom and democracy are inseparable ideas.

The Lincoln Memorial in Washington, DC, a tribute to one of the USA's great heroes. As president, Lincoln led the North to victory in the Civil War and freed most of the black slaves in the Southern states.

Lincoln on democracy

A classic definition of democracy was given by Abraham Lincoln, President of the USA (1861-84), in his Gettysburg Address. Commemorating the soldiers who had fallen in the American Civil War, he declared that they had died so that

'the government of the people, by the people, and for the people, shall not perish from the earth'.

Counting votes. The people wearing different-coloured rosettes represent rival political parties. They are present in order to make sure the count is fair.

Voting by secret ballot. This woman's ballot paper goes straight into a box with thousands of others. No one will know who she has voted for.

Types of democracy

In practice, the ideal of rule by the people is not so easy to carry out. In its purest form, a democracy would be run by meetings attended by every citizen. After examining the facts and discussing what needed to be done, the people would make the laws, decide every act of government policy and judge every dispute that arose in the community.

Such a system, known as direct democracy, could only work for a small state with few inhabitants and a simple way of life. Even if we could be sure that this was the best way of running things, it would not be practicable in the modern world, where even small countries have millions of citizens and are faced with complex problems. Instead, present-day societies, if they are democratic at all, are representative democracies. Those who make laws and govern are directly or indirectly chosen by the people through elections in which all citizens may cast their votes. The people's representatives are expected to operate in a way that benefits the community as a whole, and they can be removed from office during new elections.

Voting is necessary in democracies because groups and individuals have conflicting interests and ideas. For example, a conflict of interests occurs when one group thinks the government should help farmers, while another group wants resources used to benefit industry. A typical conflict of ideas might divide a community between people who believe in control of the economy by the state and those who think that business and markets work best when left alone.

In a democracy, politicians try to persuade people to support their policies. Here, Al Gore makes a point in a debate with George Bush (seated, right), his rival in the US presidential election held in November 2000.

Parties and elections

Conflicts of interests and ideas lead voters and their would-be representatives to organize themselves into rival groups. The would-be representatives become candidates for election, working with like-minded candidates and their supporters. This is the origin of rival political parties, which try to win over as many electors as possible to their point of view. Each party hopes that, after an election, its representatives will be more numerous than the representatives of other parties, and will be in a position to make laws, or govern, or both. Whatever the outcome, people chosen by the voters – their representatives – will hold office in, or be in authority over, the main branches of government: the executive, the legislature and the judiciary. Though democracy is possible without political parties, in practice only multi-party democracies seem to have much staying power.

Because people have conflicting interests and ideas, democracies rely heavily on voting for decision-making. The majority carries the day, whether the voting takes place at an election or in a legislative assembly. But there is always a possibility that the majority will use its power to oppress smaller groups or individuals, especially if these happen to be

Branches of government

Politics in a democracy involves three branches of government:

The legislature makes laws (legislates). It usually consists of one, or more often two, assemblies, chambers or 'houses' of representatives. The names of legislatures vary from country to country; examples include Parliament (Britain), Congress (USA) and the National Assembly (France).

The executive carries out the laws and controls the state from day to day; it is what we mean when we talk about 'the government'. It is headed by a chief executive who is generally known by a title such as prime minister, president or chancellor. He or she is in charge of a cabinet or group of ministers, each in control of a particular aspect of policy (for example, foreign affairs or transport).

The judiciary comprises the courts, judges and juries. It decides whether laws have been broken and arbitrates in disputes involving interpretation of the law. The judiciary may also have to judge whether a government's actions or regulations have gone beyond the powers granted to it by the legislature. And in states with a written constitution, the judiciary may have to decide whether a law is unconstitutional (contains provisions forbidden by the constitution).

unpopular. To take an extreme case, the legislature of a country where the majority of people belonged to Religion A might pass a law banning Religions B and C. This might be 'democratic' in a sense, but democrats in fact condemn such behaviour as 'the tyranny of the majority'. Protecting the freedom of the individual has a high priority in democracies, usually spelled out in a constitution. This is the fundamental law of the state, and often includes a list of human rights that must be respected, such as the right to personal liberty, freedom of speech and freedom of assembly. These protect the individual against the majority, and the majority against representatives who try to abuse their powers.

Constitutions

A constitution is a framework of principles, ideas and rules that lays down how a state is to be run. Most states have written constitutions – documents that define how the government should behave and how laws are to be made.

One important purpose of a constitution is to protect citizens against oppression, and so it usually puts limits on governments and laws. For example, a constitution might forbid the making of any law that was unfair to people because of their religion or ethnic origins. Even if such a law was passed by the legislature, it would still be unconstitutional (and so not valid) unless the constitution itself had been changed beforehand.

Because a constitution is such a fundamental document, an exceptional level of agreement among citizens is usually necessary before anything in it can be amended (altered). But new circumstances and ideas do arise from time to time and, for example, 27 amendments were made to the Constitution of the USA between 1791 and the end of the 20th century.

Some countries, among them the United Kingdom, are said to have unwritten constitutions. This means that they have no fundamental document that overrides all others, but that their political life is directed by laws, customs and habits that, taken together, act like a constitution.

For all these reasons democracy is an attractive form of government. And the strongest argument in its favour seems self-evidently right: if all the citizens in a community are affected by its laws, and by the actions of its government, all of them should have a say in making those laws and choosing that government.

Other systems

Yet for most of human history, democracy has been the exception, not the norm. Over long periods societies have been ruled by individuals such as monarchs and dictators, or by elites based on military prowess, noble blood, wealth or some other advantage that gave them authority over the majority of the people. This does not mean that rulers always did as they pleased, without thinking about the well-being of the majority. In many societies the way power was used was determined by traditions, laws and the existence of councils, parliaments, estates or other representative institutions – institutions that were not democratic but did speak for some part of the community and in some instances eventually developed towards democracy.

Surprisingly, both democracy and representative institutions are not centuries but thousands of years old, with their roots in the Ancient World.

Chinese protesters demand democracy in Tiananmen Square, 31 May 1995. Their 'Goddess of Democracy' faces a picture of the former communist leader Mao Zedong.

The Ancient World

Most of the early states that we know much about were monarchies, ruled by a king or emperor. Wars of conquest led to the formation of large states such as Egypt, Babylon and Persia, where everyone did the will of the Pharaohs or the Great Kings. Their despotic authority was restrained only by tradition and religion, and overthrown only as a result of assassination, revolt or civil war.

Societies of a very different kind grew up among the ancient Greeks, who lived in dozens of small political communities known as city-states. The typical city-state, or *polis*, consisted of a single city and enough surrounding countryside to feed its inhabitants. This encouraged an active, independent way of life that made the Greeks a highly creative people, and the achievements of city-states such as Athens, Sparta and

The Rule of Law

The Greeks believed their way of life made them superior to other peoples, whom they lumped together as 'barbarians'. Even the Persians, rulers of a large, wealthy and civilized empire, were dismissed as inferior. One reason for the Greek attitude was that in Persia the Great King could have a man killed on the spot. In Greek eyes that meant that the Persians were no better than slaves, whereas the Greek was a free man because the Rule of Law prevailed in the city-state. The law was known to all, and its provisions applied to all. The government might be controlled by a minority and the laws might be harsh, but those laws, and not a tyrant's whim, determined how individuals were treated. The concept of the Rule of Law has greatly influenced European thought, where it marks the vital distinction between the constitutional state, however limited the freedoms it allows, and a country ruled by a despot, or a police state, where no one can feel completely secure.

Thebes have been celebrated ever since. As well as unsurpassed contributions to literature, art and architecture, the Greeks invented the drama and pioneered the writing of history and philosophy. They were also formidable warriors who defeated huge invading Persian armies and, eventually, overthrew the mighty Persian empire.

Most citizens of a *polis* lived in the city or close enough to take part in its affairs. Over several centuries the city-states experimented with a variety of political forms, including rule by a 'strong man' and three types of government which we still describe by using the Greek words: aristocracy (rule by a noble elite), oligarchy (rule by the few) and democracy.

Greek democracy

By the 5th century BC most Greek city-states were either oligarchies or democracies. The most brilliant of the democracies was Athens, where a series of reforms changed the constitution so that even members of the poorest class, the *thetes*, were allowed to vote and to hold political office. All citizens could attend the Assembly where laws and other decisions were made, and so Athens was very close to being a direct democracy. Day-to-day affairs were in the hands of a Council of Five Hundred, which was not elected but chosen by lot – a curious but effective device that brought as many citizens as possible into government and prevented ambitious individuals or groups from dominating the council year after year. All citizens could become jurors in the courts, and since Athenian juries were very large (typically 501 members), many

One of the ways in which the ancient Greeks voted: the 'ballot paper' is a piece of broken pottery on which the voter scratched names – in this case, which politicians should be sent into exile!

11

did; there was even a small payment for service, so that the poor would not be put off by the prospect of missing a day's paid work.

All this showed an impressive belief in the ability of any citizen to perform the duties of any office. Most offices could not be held by an individual for more than a single year or two consecutive years, and this also brought in as many individuals as possible. The main exceptions were the ten *strategoi*, or 'generals', who could be elected again and again, since the Athenians realized that in military matters expertise was vital. The *strategoi* soon came to include figures who were politicians rather than generals. The most notable was Pericles, who was effectively the leader of

Pericles was Athens' leader from about 460 BC to his death from the plague in 429. This was probably the time of the city's greatest glory, when Athens commanded a league of Greek states and built the most famous of Greek temples, the Parthenon.

Praise of Athens' democracy

Pericles described the Athenian system:

'We live under a form of government that is not copied from the institutions of our fellow men but rather provides a model for others. It is known as democracy because power is exercised in the interests of the many, not the few. But while the laws give all men equal rights in their private disputes, public honours are paid to an individual on the basis of his personal qualities, not his rank or family connections; nor does poverty disqualify a man of low birth if he is capable of useful public service. We conduct ourselves as free men in our private lives too, avoiding mutual jealousies and suspicion; if our neighbour chooses to live after his own fashion, we do not resent it.'

Athens for most of his forty years in politics. But although Pericles had a powerful influence over his fellow-Athenians, as a democrat he still had to convince the Assembly that his policies were correct, and to work for the support of the majority.

A discussion at the Academy, founded by Plato in the 3rd century BC to train philosophers and statesmen; Roman mosaic.

Greek democracy had strict limits, always excluding women and slaves. And despite Athens' great achievements, the idea of democracy was not widely praised in the Ancient World. Among the weightiest objections were those put forward by two great Greek philosophers, Plato (c.427-347 BC) and Aristotle (384-322 BC), who created the world's first works of political philosophy. Plato's *Republic* pictures an ideal *polis*; he rejects democracy on the grounds that governing, like other pursuits, should be left to people with the right training and skills. Aristotle, in his *Politics*, regards democracy as an unstable form of government, likely to be exploited by demagogues – agitators who stir up the people for their own ends. It was well known that popular assemblies could be easily swayed, and on one notorious occasion the Athenian assembly voted to punish a rebellious city with great cruelty, only to change its mind the next day (the ship carrying the countermanding order arrived only just in time to prevent a massacre). The criticisms put forward by Plato and Aristotle are worth thinking about, though it is not certain that Plato's experts would have done better than the Athenian democrats.

Athens reached the height of its power as the head of the Delian League of democratic city-states, but it was eventually defeated (404 BC) by an oligarchic league led by Sparta. Democracy survived for a time in Greece, but big power-blocs soon overshadowed all the city-states, whether democracies or oligarchies, and in the mid-1st century BC they were incorporated into the great new Mediterranean empire of Rome.

Aristotle (384-322)

One of the greatest figures in the history of philosophy, Aristotle was above all an analyst and systematizer of knowledge; his writings on science, literature, ethics and politics have had an extraordinary impact on European thought. The son of a doctor, he was born at Chalcidice in northern Greece, but settled in Athens and spent twenty years studying under the older philosopher Plato. Later Aristotle established his own school, the Lyceum; many of his books are based on the courses of lectures he gave there. Aristotle's *Politics* is the first book in history to compare states with different political systems (comparative government), and contains insights into citizenship, the law, ways of achieving stability in the state and many other topics. It contains the memorable statement that 'Man is a political animal', by which he meant that the *polis* was the most natural and best framework for human activity.

The Roman Republic

Rome too had a great influence on later political thought, because the institutions of the Roman state endured for so long and also because the Romans tried to solve a number of fundamental political problems. Towards the end of the 6th century BC they drove out their king and established a republican city-state; the very word 'republic' comes from *res publica* (public matters) in Latin, the language spoken by the Romans. Rome was never a democracy, but it did have a constitution and representative institutions designed to provide a degree of freedom and stability. Executive power was entrusted to two consuls who were elected yearly; rotating the duties of the two consuls was intended to prevent either from wielding too much power and trying to become a king or tyrant. After a series of struggles between the patricians (the

Roman senators in a civic procession; this superbly carved relief sculpture is part of a 1st-century AD monument called the Ara Pacis (Altar of Peace). The members of the Senate were all men, mostly of noble birth, who had held high office in the state.

aristocratic class) and the plebeians (ordinary citizens), the plebeians were allowed to hold some public offices and the authority of the patrician-dominated assembly, the Senate, was to some extent counterbalanced by that of a popularly elected tribune who was entitled to summon a popular assembly. In this way the Romans attempted to devise a balanced constitution, a concept taken up by many later political thinkers.

Among other Roman innovations was the extension of citizenship to conquered peoples. The Athenians had viewed citizenship as a purely local privilege, not available even to other Greeks who settled in the city. By making Roman citizens of their fellow-Italians, and later of Spaniards, Gauls and other peoples, Rome reconciled the conquered and created a new idea of how an international order might operate.

The Roman Republic functioned well for several hundred years, but eventually the demands of ruling vast territories became too great. Successful generals fought one another to control the empire until Julius Caesar emerged as master of the Roman world. Caesar

The vocabulary of politics

Many of the terms we use in discussing politics come directly from the ancient Greeks and Romans. The Greeks gave us aristocracy, oligarchy and democracy; and politics itself comes from the Greek *polis*, 'city-state', and *polites*, 'a citizen'. Words of Latin origin include republic, Senate, Capitol, tribune, consul, dictator and emperor. The name of the first imperial family, Caesar, was adopted as a title by all later Roman emperors, and German and Russian versions of the word, Kaiser and Tsar, were in use down to the early 20th century.

was assassinated, but he was succeeded by his great-nephew Augustus, who became the first Roman emperor (27 BC-AD14). Although the republican forms were kept up, autocracy – rule by a single individual – again became the accepted way of governing.

Dictators

When republican Rome was in danger, a leader was chosen to deal with the emergency. Known as the dictator, he was given complete authority, including powers of life and death, over the state, army and citizens. He was appointed for a six-month term of office which could be renewed if necessary.

For a long time the system worked well, and some dictators were regarded by the Romans as heroic figures. Cincinnatus was famous for laying down his office the moment the crisis was past and going back to his farm: one day he was all-powerful, the next he was behind the plough in his own fields. Later in Roman history, as ambitious men such as Julius Caesar fought for supremacy in the republic, the winner was named dictator, and the title became no more than official recognition of where power lay.

In modern times, the Roman word 'dictator' has been widely used to describe individuals who acquire absolute power. To do so they sometimes use a real or pretended emergency, but few of them follow Cincinnatus and give it up when life returns to normal.

A modern dictator. Saddam Hussein has ruled Iraq since 1979. He was re-elected president in 1995 – possibly because anyone who opposes him is killed.

Centuries of Change

In the 5th century AD, the western part of the Roman Empire collapsed under the impact of invasions by Germanic tribes. Over the next thousand years (the Middle Ages) a new European society, and new nations such as England and France, developed. Representative institutions existed, partly stemming from the Germanic tradition of tribal assemblies, and persisted among peoples such as the Anglo-Saxons and the Vikings. Later, councils and assemblies of various kinds came into being because royal resources were limited in the new societies and a monarch needed the co-operation of important men in local communities.

The oldest parliament

Iceland's Althing is often described as the oldest surviving parliament in Europe. Apart from a few Irish hermits, the first settlers in Iceland were Norwegians who arrived from 874 onwards. By about 930 they had established the Althing, an assembly which met for two weeks every summer to pass laws and act as a court to decide legal disputes.

The Althing was dominated by chiefs, the *godar*, from a small number of leading families. Many had left Norway rather than submit to the king, so in Iceland no central government was set up – with the curious result that a man might win a favourable verdict from the court but had to enforce it himself.

After civil wars broke out between the *godar*, Iceland came under Norwegian rule (1264), then passed to Denmark (1380). The Althing remained important until the 17th century, then declined and was finally abolished in 1800. But shortly afterwards a national revival began, and in 1845 a modernized Althing met at the Icelandic capital, Reykjavik. In 1904 Iceland won virtually full independence, completed in 1944 when it became a republic.

Another influence was the feudal system, which bound together monarch, barons, churchmen, knights and serfs, encouraging the idea that superior and inferior had mutual rights and duties.

Representing the community

By the late Middle Ages, councils of powerful nobles often advised monarchs, who might also consult the wider 'community of the realm' through an assembly of the Three Estates – representatives of the nobility, the clergy and the commons (the mass of the people, from the wealthiest merchant to the landless pauper). Representing people in terms of group interests (rather than as individuals) seemed natural in static traditional societies with wide differences in status and no concept of equal citizenship.

Peasants at work getting in the harvest; a vivid little sketch from a 14th-century psalm book. Their work was vital, but like the common people for most of history, they had no political rights.

The feudal system

Medieval societies were hierarchies – pyramids of power in which, typically, a monarch occupied the apex, with greater and lesser lords and

other property-owners in ranks below him. At the bottom of the pyramid were those who worked on the land and produced the food, many of them serfs with very limited legal rights.

Such hierarchies have existed in many societies. The special feature of feudalism was that relationships were regulated by contracts. The king, who was in theory the owner of the entire realm, gave lands to his great lords, or tenants-in-chief, in return for specified services. The great lords granted smaller parcels of land to lesser lords on similar terms; and so on, level by level. Feudalism made law a central feature of social arrangements, and this helps to explain why, even when powerful monarchies emerged in Europe, rulers rarely behaved like tyrants, preferring to act within the law.

Estates and parliaments were usually called when the monarch decided they were needed, often because he or she wanted them to agree to new taxes. The Estates could then air popular grievances, and on such occasions they sometimes became – briefly – of real political importance. But in the 16th and 17th centuries much more united and centralized states developed. Over much of Europe, during this 'Age of Absolutism', monarchs became more powerful than ever before. The Estates and other assemblies were either suppressed or ceased to be of much importance.

Magna Carta

England's King John (1199-1216) was an able, domineering ruler. Disastrous foreign wars weakened his position, and in 1215 he was forced to yield to the demands of his baronial opponents. On 12 June, at Runnymede, he affixed his seal to a document known as Magna Carta (the Great Charter) which placed limits on royal power and recognized the rights and liberties of his subjects. The most famous clauses declared that the king could not levy taxes without consent; guaranteed that 'No freeman shall be taken or imprisoned, deprived of his lands, outlawed or exiled ... save by the lawful judgement of his peers or the law of the land'; and promised that justice would be available to all. John was soon fighting the barons again, but Magna Carta was constantly reissued, so that in time it came to be seen as a fundamental statement of English liberties.

The English Parliament

The most important exception was England (Great Britain from 1707; the United Kingdom, or UK, from 1801), where the representative assembly was known as Parliament. It developed in the 13th century from councils of royal advisers, which became the nucleus of the House of Lords. Representatives of the counties and towns were first summoned to Parliament in the 13th century. They began to meet as a separate body from the 14th, and eventually formed Parliament's second house or chamber, the House of Commons.

The King in Parliament. This is a 16th-century artist's idea of how an early (13th-century) meeting of Parliament looked. The enthroned King Edward I (1270-1307) dominates the proceedings, looking down on the lords (right) and the bishops (left).

Parliament's importance greatly increased in the 16th century, when it was kept busy by the Tudor king Henry VIII, passing the laws that brought about the English Reformation (the break with the Roman Catholic Church). From this time Acts of Parliament, rather than royal proclamations, became the source of new laws, laying the basis for what would eventually become the sovereignty of Parliament.

In the 17th century, when representative bodies were disappearing or becoming powerless on the continent of Europe, the English Parliament more than held its own in religious and constitutional disputes with the Stuart kings James I and Charles I. When civil war broke out, Parliament was victorious. Charles I was executed in 1648, and England became a republic – though far from a democracy, since Parliament still represented only the propertied classes. But the republican experiment was a failure, and for some years the country was effectively ruled as a military dictatorship by Oliver Cromwell.

Parliament dissolved by force: Oliver Cromwell's soldiers driving members from the building in 1653. Having defeated the king, Parliament found itself for a time at the mercy of its own armed forces. This picture was obviously the work of a Cromwellian, since he sees the occasion as a bit of a joke.

Early democrats

In the aftermath of the English Civil War, a radical movement, the Levellers, developed democratic ideas that alarmed Parliament and the army leader, Oliver Cromwell. In 1647 Cromwell took part in the Putney Debates held between army factions. One officer, Colonel Rainsborough, stood up for the Levellers. Using 'he' where we would say 'person', he told Cromwell,

'I think that the poorest he that is in England hath a life to live as the greatest he; and therefore, truly, Sir, I think it's clear that every man that is to live under government ought first by his own consent to put himself under that government.'

After Cromwell's death the monarchy was restored (1660), but Parliament kept most of the powers it had wrested from Charles I. Political and religious struggles continued until 1688, when James II went into exile and Parliament effectively appointed Queen Mary and her Dutch husband William III as joint sovereigns.

Prime minister Sir Robert Walpole with his ministers. Such 18th-century meetings, held without the king, were a step towards parliamentary government.

The Declaration of Rights, issued in 1689, guaranteed that in future there would be free elections, freedom of speech in Parliament and regular meetings of Parliament. The place of Parliament in the constitution was assured, and members' experience of working in committees and scrutinizing government accounts made it highly effective. The monarch remained powerful, but now needed to work closely with the Lords and Commons. This was especially true as rudimentary political parties developed and monarchs found that it was only possible to govern through a chief minister (soon to be called the prime minister) who was supported by the majority of Members of Parliament.

Enlightened thinker

Charles-Louis de Secondat, Baron de Montesquieu (1689-1755), was one of the outstanding thinkers of the French Enlightenment. After a career in law, he published *Persian Letters* (1721), a satire in which an imaginary Persian tourist describes French society; seen by an outsider, many political and social customs were shown to be absurd. Montesquieu's studies and travels gave him the materials for his masterpiece, *The Spirit of the Laws* (1748), which compared different states and advocated the Separation of Powers as the best way to ensure political liberty.

With its freedom of speech and attachment to the rule of law, Britain was greatly admired by 18th-century visitors such as the French thinkers Voltaire and Montesquieu. These men were part of a general intellectual movement, the Enlightenment, which judged traditional institutions by rational standards, condemning cruel and superstitious practices and advocating religious tolerance. Though democracy was not yet on the agenda, Montesquieu did argue in favour of a limited, responsible government (implicitly condemning France's absolutist system) and a balanced constitution based on the Separation of Powers.

Separation of Powers

The Separation of Powers describes the concept of making the executive, legislature and judiciary completely independent of one another and run by different personnel. In this way, no one branch of government can control the other two and abuse its power; the disadvantage of a complete separation is that the branches of government may oppose one another and paralyse the state. The doctrine of the Separation of Powers was first clearly stated by the French thinker Montesquieu. His writings strongly influenced the framing of the American constitution, in which the separation, though not complete, is very marked.

The American Revolution

New ideas and social and economic changes were soon to transform absolutist Europe. But the first crisis occurred in the British colonies of North America. The British parliamentary tradition extended to these Thirteen Colonies, which had their own assemblies and enjoyed a measure of self-government. So as self-reliant small farmers with some political experience, the colonists reacted vigorously to what they saw as unfair taxes levied by the British government. They argued that, unlike every part of Britain, the American colonies were not represented in the British Parliament at Westminster, and on this basis they coined the potent slogan 'No taxation without representation!'

Mishandled by the British government, the dispute turned into an armed conflict, and a militant section of the colonial population decided to break with Britain completely. In 1776 Thomas Jefferson drafted the Declaration of Independence which, under the influence of Enlightenment thought, identified the

Signing the Declaration of Independence, 1776. This painting is by John Trumbull, who served under George Washington and knew most of the signatories.

The Declaration of Independence

The Declaration of Independence (1776) began with a statement of human rights and the objects of government:

'We hold these truths to be self-evident, that all men are created equal, that they are endowed by their Creator with certain inalienable Rights, that among these are Life, Liberty and the pursuit of Happiness. That to secure these rights, Governments are instituted among Men, deriving their just powers from the consent of the governed ...'

welfare of the people as the object of government, and declared that the people had the right to overthrow it if it behaved tyrannically.

A year later, representatives of the former colonies (which now considered themselves independent states) signed Articles of Confederation that linked them under the name the United States. Led by George Washington, the revolutionary forces were victorious, and in 1783 the British government was forced to recognize the independence of the United States.

George Washington leading his troops across the ice-choked Delaware River on Christmas night, 1776; the night attack on Trenton that followed was one of his most famous exploits.

Thomas Jefferson (1743-1826)

One of the most admired of America's Founding Fathers, Jefferson was a greatly gifted political leader, diplomatist, writer, architect and patron of science. A Virginian, he became one of the leading lawyers in the Thirteen Colonies before joining the movement against British rule. He drafted the Declaration of Independence, and although some changes were made in his text, its noble phrases and most of the content were his.

As Secretary of State (in charge of foreign affairs; 1790-93), Vice-President (1797-1801) and President (1801-9), Jefferson opposed attempts to strengthen the executive and suppress opposition, encouraging democratic tendencies in the state. Though he failed to speak out against slavery in the USA, he has generally been recognized as a man of singular vision and integrity.

In framing a constitution for the new country, the states were unwilling to give up all their powers, so the United States became a federation; each state retained its own government and laws, granting the central, or federal, government the power to pass laws or take action in a limited range of matters of common interest. (So the USA's federal constitution differed greatly from the unitary system in Britain, where Parliament was supreme and could, if it wished, override any institution in the land.)

Federations

Federal systems suit large states, and states whose regions are widely different in character. Present-day federal states include Australia, Canada, Germany, India, Russia and the USA.

Suspicious of 'tyranny' after their experience of British rule, the makers of the Constitution devised a system of checks and balances to ensure that no individual or branch of the federal government could become too powerful. Inspired by the concept of the Separation of Powers, they arranged that no member of the executive (the president and his cabinet) could become a member of the legislature (Congress, consisting of the House of Representatives and the Senate). At the apex of the judiciary, the Supreme Court had the power to decide whether or not an executive act or law was constitutional; the Court's members, though appointed by the president, held office for life and were therefore independent.

In 1789 George Washington took office as first president of the United States. It was still far from being a democracy, but the social upheavals of the war years, and the emphasis on individual liberty in the Declaration of Independence and the Constitution, made it likely that the popular element in government would become increasingly strong.

Presidents and prime ministers

Democracies have two main types of governmental system.

In a presidential system, such as the USA's, the president (the chief executive) is elected separately from the legislature and each is independent of the other.

In Britain and other prime ministerial or cabinet systems, the prime minister is the chief executive. He or she is a member of the legislature, leads the party with the majority in it (or sometimes a coalition [alliance] of parties) and chooses the cabinet of leading ministers from it. Losing the support of the legislature will force the prime minister to resign.

Confusingly, in a republic with a prime ministerial system (e.g. Germany), the head of state is usually called the president; but this kind of president, like a constitutional monarch, is a figurehead with almost no political power.

The French Revolution

The American colonists had won their freedom with military assistance from France. But when French soldiers who had fought in America returned to their own country, they left liberty behind them. France was still an absolute monarchy, where King Louis XVI ruled by divine authority (God's will) and nobles and clergy enjoyed extraordinary rights and privileges including an almost complete exemption from taxation. But by the late 18th century new forces were at work, while the entire political and social system had become out of date. The state finances reached the point of collapse, and still the nobility and clergy refused to give up any of their privileges. Finally, in 1789, Louis XVI became desperate enough to summon a meeting of the Estates General, a half-forgotten body that had not met since 1614.

Louis hoped that the three Estates, or orders – nobles, clergy and commons – would remain docile while helping him solve his problems. Instead, the commons (the Third Estate) took a bold initiative, fusing the three Estates into a single National Assembly that claimed to represent the entire people. The Old Regime of royal authority and feudal privilege was swept away, and a Declaration of Rights was passed, proclaiming that 'The source of all sovereignty resides essentially in the nation'. Though the sentiment sounded democratic, the Assembly actually aimed to create a constitutional monarchy (that is, one where the monarch's powers were defined, and limited, by a constitution) and give the vote only to people with a certain amount of property.

The three French Estates, nobility, clergy and people, work together like blacksmiths hammering iron into shape – but what they are forging is a constitution; an illustration from the early phase of the French Revolution.

July 1789: the storming of the Bastille, a hated symbol of royal power.

This was the start of what became known as the French Revolution. Its later course was even more dramatic, as conflicts between the king, the nobles and the representatives of the people led to the declaration of a republic, the execution of Louis XVI and war between France and the rest of Europe. For a time, radical political leaders took power, and in 1793 a new constitution gave the vote to all adult males (universal male suffrage). However, the war prevented the constitution from being put into operation, and later on more conservative leaders took over. Eventually Napoleon Bonaparte established a military dictatorship and crowned himself Emperor of the French. During his spectacular career he conquered much of Europe, but his final defeat in 1815 appeared to spell the end for the Revolution and the ideas associated with it.

Right, Left and Centre

One of the legislative assemblies during the French Revolution, the Convention, met in a hall where the seats were arranged in a semi-circle. The radical deputies (representatives) gathered on the left-hand side; the conservative deputies stayed as far away from them as possible, on the right; deputies who were uncommitted, or middle-of-the-road in their views, sat in the centre. Thanks to this accidental arrangement, the Left and the Right, or left-wing and right-wing, have been used ever since to describe radicals and conservatives (those who aim to change society and those who strive to maintain the established order).

Towards Democracy

In the 19th century the tide at last began to run in favour of democracy. The pace of change varied from country to country, and in most cases full democracy was not achieved until well into the 20th century. But in the USA, the British Empire and much of Europe the trend was clear by 1900.

A new kind of society

Two important sources of the trend were the French Revolution, with its call for 'Liberty, Equality and Fraternity', and the Industrial Revolution, which, beginning in Britain, created a society based on factories and cities rather than farming and the land. In the long run there would have to be political arrangements to represent the increasingly prosperous and confident middle class and the new type of industrial working class, which was massed in cities rather than scattered over the land like farmers and peasants in pre-industrial societies. While many

Factory workers at Woolwich, London, in 1862. During the 19th century Britain became the first industrial society, an event that had important consequences for the development of democracy.

agriculturally based societies still lacked any kind of constitution, in industrial countries some of the sharpest political conflicts were about extending the franchise (that is, widening the right to vote) within an already existing constitutional system.

Slavery and freedom

In the USA the franchise was determined by individual states, and at first only male landowners could vote; however, the number of electors was relatively large, since land was cheap and abundant. Agitation to widen the franchise met with little opposition, and by the mid-19th century all adult white male Americans had the right to vote.

However, the strikingly democratic spirit of the USA was contradicted by the existence of an institution that had disappeared from Europe: slavery. The slaves were Africans, or the descendants of Africans, who had been forcibly brought to North America. There were few of them in the northern states of the USA, and slavery was soon abolished there; but in the South there were large numbers of slaves, mainly labouring on the highly productive cotton plantations. From the 1830s movements calling for the abolition of slavery became strong in the North, and tensions between North and South culminated in the Civil War of 1861-65. The defeat of the South brought the end of slavery and made black American males, at least in theory, free and equal citizens of the USA.

General Andrew Jackson in 1829, standing on a coach and waving to supporters on his way to Washington to become president of the USA. His humble origins and belief in the people, in contrast to earlier, mainly aristocratic leaders, helped to democratize American politics.

In Europe, the fall of Napoleon in 1815 did not lead to a complete restoration of the old order. Though unpopular as conquerors, Napoleon's armies had introduced many reforms, not all of which could be reversed, and the ideas of the French Revolution remained a powerful influence. For decades there were struggles in many parts of Europe between liberals, who favoured constitutions, and conservatives, who clung to the old order. Change was very slow, even after revolutions flared up over most of the continent in 1848, especially since national ambitions were often seen as more important than political liberty.

Democracy defeated: Vienna, one of the centres of the 1848 revolutions, is shown here besieged by the Austrian army. The city fell in October.

Liberal and conservative

These words have been used in a number of different and confusing ways. In the 19th century, liberals were people in favour of constitutional government and individual freedom; conservatives preferred more monarchical or aristocratic forms, or wanted to restrict the franchise to a small number of propertied voters. The liberal view has prevailed over much of the world, and countries such as the USA are often described as liberal democracies. In these, modern 'conservatives' are among the supporters of liberal democracy.

Currently 'liberal' often describes policies such as trying to help and reform convicted criminals, by contrast with the conservative emphasis on upholding law and order through stern punishments; the clash of views runs through a range of issues. 'Liberal' is also used in economic discussions to describe free-market policies (letting economic forces work themselves out without interference), as opposed to state regulation.

Battles for the vote

France underwent bewildering changes of regime until the Third Republic was established in 1871; soon afterwards, universal male suffrage was introduced. Germany, united for the first time, introduced universal male suffrage in 1871; but the German legislature, the Reichstag, had only limited control over policy, restrained by Germany's federal structure and the power and prestige of the emperor, the military and the nobility.

In the south-east European empire of Austria-Hungary, parliamentary government was frequently impossible because of the rivalries between the national groups that composed it; even the introduction of universal male suffrage in 1907 did little to alleviate its problems. Other European countries – Italy, Norway, Sweden, Denmark – completed their development towards universal male suffrage in this period.

Only the third of the European empires, vast, backward Russia, remained in theory and practice an autocracy under the Tsar, Nicholas II; after a revolutionary episode in 1905-6 it acquired an assembly, the Duma, but once Nicholas had regained control it was remodelled to represent only the wealthy and have minimal independence.

Britain shared the 19th-century impulse to liberalize society and extend the franchise. This occurred in piecemeal fashion over a century or so, without major upheavals but often in response to popular discontent. The Great Reform Bill of 1832 enfranchised the middle class, and further reforms in 1867 and 1884 gave the vote to large sections of the working class in the cities and the countryside.

The secret ballot

Being able to vote in secret is essential for genuine democracy. If you have to vote in public, people may try to make you choose the candidate they favour: for example, your employer can threaten to sack you if you refuse. In its modern form the secret ballot was introduced in two Australian states in 1856, then by Britain in 1872 and the USA after 1884.

Inheriting their political institutions from the past, the British adapted them instead of scrapping them. The powers of the monarch were whittled away, and eventually it was established that he or she would always act on the advice of the prime minister; so any special ('prerogative') powers retained by the monarch were in fact exercised by the prime minister, who as head of the largest party in the House of Commons was, in effect, elected by the voters. The unelected

Jeremy Bentham (1748-1832)

A British lawyer and reformer, Jeremy Bentham put forward a philosophy known as Utilitarianism (from utility, meaning usefulness). He argued that the object of all activity, including legislation, should be to secure 'the greatest happiness of the greatest number', and even claimed that degrees of happiness could be calculated with scientific precision.

Bentham's doctrine was open to theoretical objections, but his emphasis on government action for maximum social benefit was a positive force, contrasting sharply with views of government as designed to uphold the existing social order or make the state strong. In a general sense, most modern democratic governments can be said to be utilitarian in outlook, attempting the difficult task of weighing the needs of different groups and adopting the policy that seems to produce the widest benefit.

Bentham's followers, often called philosophical radicals, were prominent in the reforms of the Poor Laws and other 19th-century British institutions.

House of Lords was able to block legislation passed by the Commons until 1911, after which it had only a two-year delaying power. In this and other ways Britain, while holding on to ancient institutions and traditional ceremonies, moved towards a system where political decisions were made by the elected representatives of the people.

The Queen's Speech, made at the state opening of Parliament. Tradition puts the peers (lords), once the most important group in Parliament, at the front.

Second chambers

In a democracy, it might seem logical for the people to elect their representatives to a single-chamber legislature. In some countries, for example New Zealand, this is so. But most democratic countries have two chambers.

In federal systems, the second chamber generally represents the interest of the states or provinces; in the USA, for example, each state, regardless of size, elects two individuals to sit in the Senate. In Britain, the House of Lords exists for historical reasons, although both its powers and the number of hereditary peers (lords) have been reduced. Its continued existence has been justified on the grounds that it holds up rash decisions, giving the Commons time for second thoughts. Similar arguments have been used in favour of second chambers elsewhere, whose members are often retired politicians and other experienced, and presumably wise, figures.

Ideas of representative government began to make an impact outside the USA and Europe. The Spanish and Portuguese colonies in Central and South America became independent and constitutional forms were adopted. But the political situation remained unstable and revolutions and military dictatorships often occurred. Elsewhere, large areas of the world had come under European control. The British and French possessed particularly large colonial empires. However, following their usual practice, British governments quickly established representative institutions and in many colonies encouraged the inhabitants to run their own affairs. This liberal policy applied to colonists who were white settlers or their descendants, but not to native peoples. But, though flawed by racism, British policy did spread the idea of democracy, and Canada, Australia, New Zealand and South Africa became effectively independent by the early 20th century.

Two pioneer leaders of the American women's suffrage movement, shown in old age: Elizabeth Cady Stanton and Susan B. Anthony (seated). They lived to see some states give women the vote, but women's suffrage became part of the constitution only in 1920.

The women's struggle

Most of the 19th century's battles over political liberty were fought by, and for the benefit of, men. Women's rights were not seen as an issue, since women were supposed to be the weaker sex, naturally inferior to men and under their guardianship. This view was thousands of years old, and not even the most daring of ancient Greek philosophers had suggested that women might be men's equals. Whether they were seen as feather-brained and irresponsible, or too good and pure to be exposed to brute realities, the conclusion was the same: women's place was in the home, and it was 'unfeminine' to be interested in politics, ideas or business.

Consequently, in the 19th century women had to struggle for legal rights, and educational and career opportunities, as well as political recognition. Apart from a few isolated radical voices, the first demands

for women's suffrage began in mid-century, formulated in the USA at the Seneca Falls Convention organized by Lucretia Mott and Elizabeth Cady Stanton, who had become politically aware through their experiences in the anti-slavery movement. A long agitation followed, led by Stanton, Susan B. Anthony and Lucy Stone. Some states were persuaded to give women the vote, but it became clear that national change would only be achieved by an amendment to the US Constitution. Between 1912 and 1919 the militant wing of the women's movement used mass demonstrations and, occasionally, obstructive tactics and hunger strikes to put pressure on Congress, while moderates used more conventional methods. In 1920, the Nineteenth Amendment to the Constitution became law and American women achieved the same political rights as men.

Militancy

In Britain the struggle was more dramatic. The first petition for women's suffrage was presented to Parliament in 1867 by a leading thinker, John Stuart Mill, whose *On the Subjection of Women* (1869) has become a classic text. Little progress was made (not least because of the hostility of a woman, Queen Victoria) despite decades of legal agitation under the leadership of Millicent Fawcett. In 1903 a new organization, the Women's Political and

Susan B. Anthony (1820-1906)

Susan Brownell Anthony was born of Quaker stock in Massachusetts. She became a schoolteacher in New York, where she submitted a successful petition for women's property rights (control over their earnings and guardianship of their children). As an agitator against slavery and for women's suffrage, she often faced hostile audiences, and her attempts to vote led to her being arrested and fined. Anthony was president of the National Woman Suffrage Association from 1892 until her retirement at the age of 80. Her periodical *The Revolution* bore the motto 'The true republic – men, their rights and nothing more; women, their rights and nothing less'.

Wicked Women

In 1868 Queen Victoria wrote to Theodore Martin that she was:

'most anxious to enlist everyone who can speak or write or join in checking this mad, wicked folly of "Women's Rights" with all its attendant horrors ... Lady Amberley [who had given a talk on female suffrage] ought to get a good whipping.'

Votes for Women!

Some examples of where and when women first won the right to vote in national elections:

1893	New Zealand	1919	Germany, Sweden, Italy
1902	Australia	1920	USA
1906	Finland	1928	Britain
1913	Norway	1944	France
1917	Soviet Russia	1949	India
1918	Canada, Denmark,	1956	Pakistan
	Britain (women over 30)	1971	Switzerland

Social Union (WPSU), was formed by Emmeline Pankhurst, and its members – 'suffragettes' – turned to militant tactics. Political meetings were disrupted, women chained themselves to the railings of the prime minister's residence, and in 1913 Emily Davison threw herself in front of the king's horse during the Derby (a famous race) and was killed. The government reacted harshly to the hunger strikes staged by arrested suffragettes, and a bitter conflict developed. During the First World War the WPSU called off its campaign; after it, the British and US governments claimed to have been convinced by women's war work that they deserved the vote. In Britain, typically, the change was introduced cautiously, in two stages: women over 30 were enfranchised in 1918, followed in 1928 by women over 21, at that time the voting age for men.

The USA and Britain were not the first states to give the vote to women, but the intensity of the struggles there made them landmarks in what appeared to be the final triumph of democracy.

Arresting a dangerous agitator: a member of the Women's Political and Social Union is taken into custody during a demonstration outside Buckingham Palace, London, in May 1914.

Ideas in Conflict

The First World War of 1914-18 was a terrible ordeal for civilization in which millions of people perished. But its end appeared to be a triumph for democracy. Leading the USA into the conflict in 1917, President Woodrow Wilson declared that 'The world must be made safe for democracy', and following the wartime collapse of the German, Austro-Hungarian and Russian empires, defeated Germany became a republic and a cluster of new states appeared in Eastern Europe and the Baltic, all more or less committed to democracy. Women were enfranchised in most of the new states, as well as in the USA and Great Britain. Democracy was not universal (especially in colonial Africa and Asia), but it now seemed to be universally recognized as the most desirable form of government.

Socialism and communism

Meanwhile the most important development in the European democracies was the rise of political parties representing the industrial working class. With names such as the Social Democratic Party, the Socialist Party and the Labour Party, these aimed to improve workers' conditions and, in the longer term, to change the economic system: capitalism, in which industries and other forms of productive wealth were privately owned and run for profit, would be replaced by socialism, in which resources would belong to the community and goods and services would be fairly distributed. Socialists argued that political democracy was meaningless unless it went along with economic democracy: that is, a distribution of wealth that provided a reasonable standard of living and adequate education, security and leisure for all.

Woodrow Wilson in about 1915, two years after becoming president of the USA. In 1917 he took the USA into the First World War, and he was the dominant figure in the peace settlements which, though flawed, were based on ideas of democracy and the right of nations to determine their own destinies.

Socialist ideas developed in response to the poverty and squalor in which workers (women and children as well as men) lived during the 19th-century Industrial Revolution. Capitalism seemed to mean that factory owners and other capitalists became rich by exploiting workers, who were paid barely enough to live on and were thrown out and left to starve as soon as trade fell off. Socialist ideas took many forms, but those of Karl Marx were particularly influential. He insisted that the capitalist class would never give up their power voluntarily, so the workers would have to overthrow existing states through revolutionary violence.

Marx's view influenced the earliest working-class parties that succeeded in gaining a mass following, notably the German Social Democrats. But as working-class conditions improved and such parties

Karl Marx (1818-83)

A radical journalist, Karl Marx was active in France, Belgium and his native Germany. After the failure of the 1848 revolutions in Europe he fled to London, where he spent the rest of his life. In collaboration with his friend Friedrich Engels (1820-95), Marx wrote *The Communist Manifesto* (1848); its famous slogan was 'Workers of all lands, unite! You have nothing to lose but your chains.' Marx's writings, including his famous *Das Kapital* (*Capital*; 1867-94), provided the basis for a philosophy of history and a programme of action that would, he predicted, culminate in the destruction of capitalism and the establishment of a socialist, and finally a classless, communist society. Marx's influence was relatively small in his lifetime but became enormous in the course of the 20th century.

took their place within the parliamentary system, many socialists became convinced that the changes they wanted could be brought about peacefully, by winning elections and making new laws. And in fact, by the early 20th century, some governments in advanced economies had begun to provide free education and some welfare benefits (such as old age pensions and unemployment insurance), though economic inequality remained deeply entrenched.

The division between parliamentary and revolutionary socialists was sharpened by the events of the First World War. Revolutions in 1917 overthrew the Russian tsar and brought to power the Bolsheviks, later known as communists, who believed in the revolutionary doctrines of Marx. After a savage civil war, the communists managed to take control of much of the old Russian empire, which became known as the USSR or Soviet Union. The Soviet Communist Party was the only political party allowed to function, but admirers of the new state claimed that it was more genuinely democratic than capitalist countries because the privileges brought by wealth had vanished and a more just and equal society was being created. Revolutionary socialists took the Soviet Union as their model, usually breaking with parliamentary socialists and forming separate communist parties.

Vladimir Ilyich Lenin, leader of the 1917 Bolshevik Revolution in Russia, making a speech in Moscow. Admirers of the new Russia (later the Soviet Union) believed that its foundation marked the beginning of a new era.

The challenge of fascism
Struggling to overcome its backwardness, the USSR posed no immediate threat to other countries. However, fear of communism created sympathy for

movements that were both anti-communist and anti-democratic. The first to seize power, in politically chaotic Italy, was the Fascist Party led by Benito Mussolini; for this reason 'fascism' is used to describe all movements of this type, despite their dissimilarities.

Fascism was nationalistic and militaristic, praising war and struggle and making a cult of leadership and obedience; uniformed militias and street violence were prime fascist tactics in their quest for power. To many people, a dictator like Mussolini seemed more dynamic than democratic presidents and prime ministers who had to work through compromises. And when democratic Europe was plunged into an economic crisis, the Great Depression that began in 1929, the appeal of fascism widened. In 1933 Adolf Hitler led the Nazi Party to power in Germany, adding poisonous racial hatreds to the fascist formula. Within a few years, more or less fascist regimes were established in Spain and Japan, Hitler was making spectacular territorial gains, and some people believed that democracy was finished and 'the fascist era' had begun.

Fascist rhetoric

From Hitler's book *Mein Kampf* (1924):

'Nature ... puts living creatures on this globe and watches the free play of forces. She then confers the master's right on her favourite child, the strongest in courage and industry ... The stronger must dominate and not blend with the weaker, thus sacrificing his own greatness. Only the born weakling can view this as cruel.'

Adolf Hitler, leader of Nazi Germany, being greeted with rapture by his followers.

In the event, Hitler's aggressions led to the Second World War (1939-45) and an alliance between the democratic western states and the Soviet Union that destroyed Nazi Germany and Fascist Italy. Looking back, the 'fascist era' was a short-lived episode, lasting less than 25 years. But it did show that democracy could become fragile if it failed to deliver good government, security or reasonable prosperity.

Cold War

Soviet-style communism had a longer run. Unlike fascism, it claimed to be a rival and superior form of democracy to the liberal or capitalist democracies. After the Second World War, Soviet troops drove the Nazis out of Eastern Europe and in most places imposed 'People's Democracies' on the population. Communism also triumphed in China, where the revolution had a genuine popular basis. World affairs were now dominated by two power blocs, the liberal-democratic West and the communist East. For 45 years the two sides waged the Cold War (so called because hostilities were intense but always fell short of a 'hot', shooting war). It ended only in 1989-91 with the collapse of the Eastern European People's Democracies and the Soviet Union.

Soviet-style communism did have a number of achievements to its credit. It turned backward Russia

Pseudo-democracy

A new Soviet constitution adopted in 1936 was claimed to be the most advanced and democratic in the world, giving not only equal political rights to all the peoples of the USSR but also the rights to work, to rest, and to material security in sickness and old age. In reality the political rights were worthless. Arrests and treason trials peaked in the 1930s, and possibly subversive national groups were deported *en masse*. An episode of this sort suggests that democracy involves much more than written rights and guarantees.

Soviet tanks in Budapest, the capital of Hungary, in 1956. When the Hungarians revolted against their communist government, they were crushed by a Soviet invasion. By this time the ideals of communism seemed remote from its reality.

into a modern industrial power. It created a welfare system that protected people from the worst effects of poverty, although the general standard of living remained low. During the 1930s these facts seemed all the more impressive because many millions in the West were jobless and desperate as a result of the Great Depression. The Soviet Union and European communist parties were also admired as being resolutely anti-fascist at a time when Britain and France seemed unwilling or unable to oppose Hitler, Mussolini and their allies.

But behind its socialist-democratic front, the communist state was deeply flawed. At its worst, one-party rule, enforced by secret police, made it possible for an individual to exercise dictatorial power. In the Soviet Union this was done by Joseph Stalin from the 1920s until his death in 1953, during which time millions of real or imagined opponents were arrested and either executed or sent for years to brutally run labour camps. Later Soviet leaders were far less bloodthirsty, but the USSR remained a one-party state where only the views of government were made known through the press and television, and where any serious form of dissent was censored or punished. Moreover, in the long run the system didn't work. The

Communist Party, supposedly 'the vanguard of the working class', became riddled with privilege and corruption. The economic system, a 'command economy' in which all decisions were taken at the centre, proved too inflexible to cope with new technological developments and, in the absence of criticism or initiative, stagnated. Finally, a huge military and diplomatic effort was made to compete with the USA; its crippling cost undermined even the positive achievements of the Soviet Union. When a reforming leader, Mikhail Gorbachev, took charge in 1985, his efforts only speeded up the collapse of the system and the break-up of the USSR.

The western democracies' encounters with fascism and communism served to highlight some of their strengths and weaknesses. Democracies were vulnerable during periods of political confusion and economic insecurity, but the fact that their governments were accountable – had to submit their records to voters, who had the power to dismiss them – was a source of strength, restricting the abuse of power and the spread of corruption. However, it was recognized that existing democracies were far from perfect, and a search for the most suitable models continued through the 20th and into the 21st century.

November 1989: joyful East Berliners flood through a gap in the Berlin Wall. The following year saw the reunification of East and West Germany. But many East Germans found that the victory of democracy involved losing communist welfare benefits, and not necessarily getting a share of western prosperity.

The Continuing Struggle

All through the Cold War, western-style democracy seemed securely established in North America, non-communist Europe and Australasia. Apart from the countries occupied by the Soviet army, the defeated states of the Second World War - West Germany, Austria, Italy and Japan - adopted democratic constitutions which worked well. In these and other democracies, parties representing different economic philosophies coexisted, and over the following half-century there were fluctuations in the popularity of semi-socialist and welfare policies on the one hand and free-market solutions on the other. (One emphasized state intervention in the economy, higher taxes and greater benefits for the disadvantaged; the other kept taxes low and relied on competition and private initiatives to create prosperity for all.) From a democratic point of view, what mattered was that the parties on both sides were prepared to accept the verdict of the electors and, if need be, to allow their opponents to govern.

The post-colonial world

The situation was far less stable in Asia and Africa, where large numbers of new states came into being in the 30 years after the Second World War. During this period almost all of the colonies that belonged to Britain, France and other European powers were given – or managed to take – their independence. The European powers had often tried to justify their rule by claiming that they were preparing their colonies for independence, but events

General Sese Seko Mobutu, who came to power in the former Belgian Congo after five years of post-colonial turmoil; his regime, though increasingly corrupt and tyrannical, lasted from 1965 until 1997.

47

showed that they had not done enough. Parliamentary regimes were set up in the colonies by the departing powers, but few survived for long. In their place, charismatic leaders set up dictatorships, often in the form of one-party states, or army commanders took power, thrusting politicians aside while accusing them (often justifiably) of corruption and incompetence; and sometimes countries sank into ruinous civil wars.

There were many reasons for these developments, among the most common being mass poverty and ignorance (and lack of the resources needed to remedy them), political inexperience, and ethnic and regional hostility. This tended to confirm the view that democracy could not work properly without a reasonably educated and prosperous electorate, enough competent politicians and officials, and a general tolerance of political opponents and groups with different beliefs or habits. But there were exceptions. Despite its enormous size and population, India functioned as a democracy from its foundation in 1947, with one brief period (1975-77) when Mrs Indira Gandhi's government ruled through emergency powers. This was a controversial episode, but the government did voluntarily end the emergency and allow a return to normal politics – something rarely seen in the impoverished 'Third World'.

Elections in India, the world's largest democracy. In this 1998 photograph the balloons carry the colours of Congress, the party that dominated Indian politics until the 1990s. Political change has been orderly, but recently religious conflicts have threatened stability.

Struggles and victories

One of the worst failings of US democracy was removed in the 1950s and '60s, when black people achieved political equality in the Southern states where they had been slaves before the Civil War. Though promised equality by amendments to the Constitution, in a number of states they were segregated (forced to use separate bus seating, park benches, etc) and excluded from political activity by a combination of intimidation and legal devices such as literacy tests and gerrymandering. As so often in American history, there were intense debates about the extent to which the federal government was allowed to intervene in the affairs of individual states. But eventually a series of Supreme Court decisions and Civil Rights acts, given practical effect through a mass movement led by Martin Luther King Jr, ended segregation

Martin Luther King Jr was a powerful speaker and a fearless non-violent leader. He was still campaigning to end prejudice and poverty when he was assassinated, aged 39, in 1968.

⭐ Gerrymandering

This describes drawing the boundaries of electoral districts in a way that produces an unfair result. One trick is to make sure that the opposition's strength is concentrated in a few districts so that it will do badly everywhere else. For example, if each of parties A and B is supported by about 50 per cent of the voters, unscrupulous boundary drawing might create eight electoral districts, in two of which B would have 10-1 majorities. Consequently A would win by about 8-5 in the remaining six districts, gaining six seats to B's two. During the period from 1920 when Northern Ireland was effectively self-governing, gerrymandering was used by the ruling Unionist authorities to make sure that, even in predominantly republican areas such as the city of Derry, the majority of local councillors were Unionists.

American dream

On 28 August 1963, at the March for Jobs and Freedom on Washington, Martin Luther King Jr made a speech that inspired a generation. Its most famous passage began:

'I still have a dream. It is deeply rooted in the American dream. I have a dream that one day this nation will rise up and live out the true meaning of its creed: "We hold these truths to be self-evident, that all men are created equal." I have a dream that one day on the red hills of Georgia, the sons of former slaves and the sons of former slave owners will be able to sit down together at the table of brotherhood ... I have a dream that my four little children will one day live in a nation where they will not be judged by the color of their skin but by the content of their character. I have a dream today.'

and asserted black voting rights. Although the problem of black poverty remained, black people in the South now took part in politics and soon began, as a matter of course, to hold various state offices.

The collapse of Soviet and East European communism in 1989-91 had worldwide effects. The former communist countries adopted the western multi-party political model and began to abandon the Soviet-style command economy. The change was often painful, especially when it meant the loss of benefits such as guaranteed jobs. In Russia, the heart of the former Soviet Union, living standards plunged disastrously; but even here, although presidential powers and government control over the media were greater than in most multi-party states, a democratic framework survived.

Russian president Boris Yeltsin and his supporters on 19 August 1991, defying politicians who tried to seize control of the USSR and end reforms. Yeltsin mobilized the people and democracy prevailed.

The failure of communism discredited the one-party state and so encouraged Third World 'pro-democracy' movements, which won rapid victories in Ethiopia, Tanzania, Togo, Zambia, Malawi and elsewhere. In South Africa, apartheid (segregation) and domination by the white minority crumbled between 1990 and 1994, when the country's first elections based on universal suffrage were held.

Successes like these suggested that multi-party democracy was the most suitable political system for a modern state, and that rival systems were bound to disappear in the long run. But democracy remained the exception in large areas of the Middle East, where one-party states

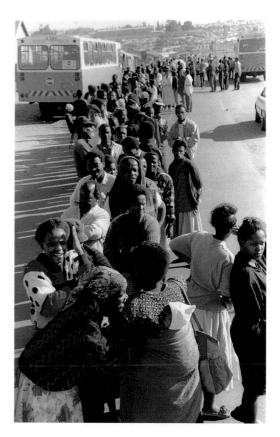

Free at last: on 27 April 1994 residents of Soweto queue to vote for the first time in their lives following the collapse of South Africa's white-dominated political system.

and traditional monarchies were more common. In the case of Iraq, which in 1990 invaded Kuwait on the orders of the Iraqi dictator Saddam Hussein, even severe military punishment by an international coalition failed to bring down the regime. Middle Eastern politics were further complicated by what the West calls Islamic Fundamentalism, the tendency of the main religion in the region, Islam, to become a political force where western and communist-style policies failed to improve conditions. In 1979 the first and most thoroughgoing Islamic revolution took place in Iran, amid great popular enthusiasm. In 1997 the election of President Khatami showed that people wished for fewer restrictions on individual freedom, but the conservative religious establishment responded by shutting down newspapers and magazines that favoured change, leaving a tense situation.

The struggle for democracy continued to produce heroic and self-sacrificing individuals such as Aung San Suu Kyi in Myanmar (Burma). In China the Communist Party kept its political monopoly, punishing pro-democracy agitation. In 1989 protests climaxed in and around Tiananmen Square, the centre of the Chinese capital, Beijing, where demonstrators erected a gigantic Goddess of Liberty that was clearly modelled on the American Statue of Liberty. The brutal reaction of the Chinese army led to heavy loss of life, and over the next few years international pressure failed to change the regime's attitude.

Ethnic conflicts

Democracy functions best in an atmosphere of mutual respect or tolerance, and so the ethnic hostilities that still occurred late in the 20th century were disturbing; some commentators felt that they were actually on the increase. Massacres in Burundi and Rwanda (1988-94) were a reminder that tribal hatreds were still alive in parts of Africa. The Tamil 'Tigers' in Sri Lanka fought to separate their community from the majority Sinhalese, and in southern Russia the Chechens' attempts to secede involved them in two devastating conflicts with the Russian army. More openly intolerant attitudes appeared in India with a rise in Hindu nationalism (Hinduism is the majority

Aung San Suu Kyi (1945-)

The daughter of one of Myanmar's national heroes, Aung San Suu Kyi married a university teacher and lived in Britain until 1988. She returned to Myanmar to look after her mother and became involved in agitation against the military who had ruled since the early 1960s. When elections were allowed in 1990, she was already under house arrest but led the National League for Democracy (NLD) to an overwhelming victory. The military ignored the result, persecuted the NLD, and only released Aung San Suu Kyi in 1995. Meanwhile, in 1991 she was awarded the Nobel Peace Prize. Her movements continued to be restricted but her persistent upholding of democratic rights won her the admiration of the world.

religion); in 1992 there was widespread violence as the 16th-century Muslim mosque at Ayodhya was deliberately destroyed, and from 1998 the Hindu nationalist Bharatiya Janata Party was in government, with as yet unpredictable consequences.

In Europe, the break-up of Yugoslavia in 1991 led to civil war in the former province of Bosnia, which had a mixed population of Serbs, Croats and Muslims. The scale of the atrocities committed, especially though not exclusively by the Serbs, gave rise to a new term, 'ethnic cleansing', used to describe systematic attempts to kill entire populations or drive them out of a region. The slaughter was ended only in 1996, through an internationally imposed settlement. A further conflict in 1998-99 came to a climax when Serbian domination of Kosovo (where 90 per cent of the province's population were Albanian) was broken by an international bombing campaign.

Ethnic issues surfaced, somewhat less intensely, in many western countries, often showing themselves in hostility towards immigrant workers and asylum-seekers. The most serious conflict, measured by loss of life, was between the Protestant-Unionist and Catholic-Republican communities of Northern Ireland. After almost thirty years of violence, peace seemed to be on the horizon in the late 1990s. The solution was a 'power-sharing' arrangement which involved both communities; it suggested that normal majority-rule democracy (which would have left power exclusively in Protestant hands) might not be the best solution to problems of this kind.

The people's will: smoke rises from the Yugoslav parliament building in Belgrade, stormed in October 2000 by Serb protesters who forced their former leader, Slobodan Milosevic, to give up power after losing the presidential election.

Issues of Today

Although one-party states, dictatorships and absolute monarchies still exist, the number of multi-party democracies has steadily increased and now includes all the world's most powerful states except China. No serious alternative seems likely to appear in the foreseeable future. But there is fierce argument about which models of democracy are best suited to modern conditions, and the complexities of the international economy have thrown up many new problems.

The method used to elect members of the legislature is of vital importance. The 'first-past-the-post' and Proportional Representation (PR) systems each have their champions, and opinions about them fluctuate violently. In 1993, following revelations of widespread corruption, the PR principle was partly abandoned in Italy; yet by the late 1990s it seemed possible that a PR element would be introduced into the UK system.

No electoral change seemed likely to break the ever-closer links between big money and politics. Huge sums were spent on electioneering, making candidates (and parties) reliant on donations from wealthy sponsors; inevitably the sponsors were suspected of receiving 'favours' when the candidate took office. Presidential campaigns in the USA were sometimes said to be no more than contests in spending, especially on TV advertising, and 'third-party' candidates were handicapped by their inability to afford media time and space.

Flawed democracy. In the US election of 2000, Ralph Nader was the Green Party candidate. He drew bigger crowds than his rivals but was kept off TV and outspent by the major parties. He received two million votes.

Electoral systems

When people vote for legislatures in first-past-the-post systems, the country is divided into electoral districts, or constituencies, and in each of these the candidate who receives the most votes is declared elected. In practice, first-past-the-post favours the big parties, often giving a party with (say) 40 per cent of the votes more than 50 per cent of the seats, so that it can govern alone; by contrast, smaller parties are disadvantaged. Various schemes of Proportional Representation produce a result that more accurately reflects voters' party preferences. On the other hand, first-past-the-post generally produces strong, stable governments, whereas PR encourages parties to multiply and often forces them to make compromises, and possibly shady deals, to create coalition governments.

A rare but important distortion in the US system occurred during the 2000 presidential election. US voters do not elect the president directly, but send representatives to vote on their behalf in an electoral college. The presidential candidate who receives most votes in a state receives all the state's electoral college votes. Though not strictly fair, this has seldom affected the result. In 2000, however, more Americans voted for Democrat Al Gore than for Republican George Bush, but Bush had a majority in the electoral college. Despite long legal wrangles, Bush became president.

Disillusion?

In the late 1990s there were signs of disillusion, perhaps not with democracy but certainly with politicians. This was partly because of funding and other scandals in the USA, the UK, France, Germany and Italy and partly because the promises on which governments were elected were broken often enough for the motoring term 'U-turn' to enter British politics. U-turns happened when policies proved expensive or unpopular, but politicians were also accused of being too influenced by pressure groups, especially those representing wealthy interests such as arms manufacturers and the tobacco industry.

Another feeling was that governments were becoming increasingly remote from their citizens, and that important decisions were hard to influence or even find out about. Governments often refused to supply information on the grounds of national security (the need to keep secrets from an enemy), although the danger involved was sometimes hard to imagine.

The sheer complexity of government also made it harder to keep under democratic control. Checks on government actions did exist, notably committees of the legislature which could mount investigations and summon ministers for questioning; and opposition parties were only too glad to denounce mistakes and abuses. But there were limits to their reach. Legislation gave ministers wide powers to take decisions and make regulations, many of which were passed on to appointed individuals or bodies. In Britain such bodies are known as quangos (quasi-autonomous non-governmental organizations) and control important areas of national life; yet unlike ministers, quangos are not elected and not accountable for what they do.

Political parties effectively accepted these criticisms when, in the late 1990s, they started to promise greater accountability and 'transparency' or 'open government'. Freedom of Information acts giving greater access to records were seen as one solution.

The media

The role of the media as guardians of democracy has been controversial. The drive to win more readers or a larger audience encourages newspapers and TV channels to uncover sensational facts. So, even if politically sympathetic to the government, a paper will generally go ahead and expose a scandal or abuse of power. But for the same reason it may be tempted to oversimplify or trivialize issues, or make a cult of celebrity and intrude grossly on people's private lives. Laws and codes of conduct have not so far succeeded

A sham?

The US novelist and political commentator Gore Vidal declared in a 1982 interview:

'Democracy is supposed to give you the illusion of choice, like Painkiller X and Painkiller Y. But they're both just aspirin.'

in eliminating this kind of activity without weakening the media's watchdog role. The fact remains that 'investigative journalism' has had major triumphs, playing a key role in unravelling the Watergate affair (which led to the resignation of US president Richard Nixon in 1974) and such funding scandals as the one in Germany that engulfed the ex-Chancellor Helmut Kohl and his Christian Democratic Party in 1999.

Apathy and involvement

On occasion the apathy of voters has caused alarm. In the USA, only about half the electorate vote for a presidential candidate. In European states the turnout at general elections is higher, but in the UK local elections arouse little interest; nor do elections to the European Parliament, reflecting British uncertainties about the political role of the European Union.

Various attempts have been made to involve people more directly in the political process, from making voting compulsory (as in Australia) to holding frequent referendums to decide individual issues; among recent

Danes demonstrating during the referendum campaign over membership of the single European currency (Euro). The result showed how independent-minded voters can be: in October 2000 they voted No, although almost all the leading Danish politicians and the media were in favour of entry.

Referendums

In a referendum or plebiscite, citizens vote on a single issue such as whether or not to adopt a constitutional change. Past misuse of referendums by dictatorial regimes made democracies suspicious of them, but in recent years they have been held quite often and the results suggest that voters are not so easily browbeaten. Referendums can be used only for a restricted range of single-issue decisions, where the result would not throw a range of government policies into confusion.

proposals are electronic voting and the installation of polling booths in supermarkets. There have also been attempts to bring government closer to people through devolution, transferring some central government powers to regions or localities. In 1999 devolved parliaments were set up for Scotland and Wales in the UK, and in 2000 similar rights were being given to Corsica, a French island with a special ethnic character.

Popular protest

When people find ordinary political activity too slow or frustrating, they may lose interest or may react in the opposite way, by taking direct action. In recent years protesters have often adopted non-violent, though not always strictly legal, tactics; when violence does on occasion flare up, there is usually a dispute about whether the blame lies with aggressive policing or a troublemaking minority. Protests of this kind may have nothing to do with loyalties to the Right or Left: in the UK, many outraged Conservatives joined demonstrations against the then Conservative govern-ment's Poll Tax (1990), which was eventually withdrawn. Over many parts of Europe in 2000, road hauliers forced go-slows on busy roads and blocked refineries in protest against high fuel prices. Other examples of direct action attempt to change wider policy, notably on the environment, as in the destruction of genetically modified crops by protesters. Such actions raise important issues for democracy, as the right to resist dictation from above and the wrong of undermining an elected government are finely balanced.

Popular protest. In September 2000, truckers created traffic jams in central London and blockaded oil depots, causing petrol shortages. They were protesting against high fuel costs and taxes.

Poverty and globalization

The fate of democracies is always bound up with issues of wealth and poverty. At the end of the 20th century the West was immensely prosperous, yet most western countries still had a large, impoverished and poorly educated 'underclass'. Globally the situation was more extreme, with millions underfed and Third World governments too deep in debt to make progress without help. As well as creating human misery, these conditions made it hard for democracy to thrive. Western-dominated institutions such as the World Trade Organization, the International Monetary Fund and the World Bank laid down economic policies that Third World countries had to follow, provoking surprisingly large protests in 1999-2000 by people demanding the democratization of the institutions and the cancellation of the debts. By contrast, the most democratic of international institutions, the United Nations, struggled to exercise any real authority.

Other large organizations tended to be regarded with suspicion. Criticism of the European Union for lack of accountability seemed confirmed in 1999 when the entire European Commission resigned following corruption scandals. But whereas the EU could be reformed, 'globalization' was seen by some as the greatest threat to democracy. Driven by profit and able to shift their operations from country to country, huge international corporations were said to be beyond the control of any government and able to use their economic power to bend states to their will. Only the future will show whether this was capitalism spinning out of control, or just a temporary state of affairs, to be sensibly adjusted by cooperative international effort.

Clearly much still needs to be done to create a fully democratic world. But in the 20th century democracy overcame great challenges; so there is reason to believe that it can do so again in the 21st century.

Two Cheers

In a 1951 essay the British novelist E. M. Forster did not give democracy three cheers, but did write:

'Two cheers for Democracy: one because it admits variety and two because it permits criticism.'

Date List

BC

510 Rome becomes a republic.

507–462 Athens becomes a democracy.

469–429 Pericles is the leading figure in democratic Athens.

431–404 Peloponnesian War ends with the defeat of Athens.

146 Greek city-states conquered by Rome.

27 Augustus becomes Emperor, effectively ending the Roman Republic.

AD
5th century Collapse of the western Roman Empire.

6th–15th centuries The Middle Ages.

c.930 Icelandic parliament, the Althing, established.

1215 Magna Carta issued.

13th century Beginnings of the English Parliament.

16th century Parliament plays vital role in the English Reformation.

1647 Putney Debates: Rainsborough argues that all men should have political rights.

1648 Charles I executed by victorious English Parliamentarians.

1688 The 'Glorious Revolution': James II exiled, William and Mary become sovereigns.

1689 Parliamentary freedoms assured by the Declaration of Rights.

1748 Montesquieu's *Spirit of the Laws* founds the study of comparative government.

1776 American colonies issue the Declaration of Independence.

1783 Independence of USA recognized.

1788 US Constitution adopted.

1789 Calling of the Estates General in France. Beginning of the French Revolution.

1793 France: a constitution framed by the Convention is the first to give the vote to all men.

1832 Britain: the Great Reform Bill gives the vote to the middle class.

1848 Revolutions in Europe. Seneca Falls Convention: beginning of US women's agitation for the vote.

1856 Secret ballot introduced in Australia.

1861–65 American Civil War.

1867 Britain: second Reform Act. J. S. Mill presents the first petition for women's suffrage.

1871 Universal male suffrage in Germany, soon followed by France.

1884 Britain: third Reform Act.

1893 New Zealand becomes the first country to give women the vote.

1911 Britain: veto of the House of Lords reduced to two-year delaying power.

1914–18 First World War.

1918 Women over thirty can vote in Britain.

1920	Nineteenth Amendment to the Constitution gives American women the vote.
1928	Britain: all adult women granted the vote.
1929	Beginning of the Great Depression.
1939–45	Second World War, ending in total defeat of fascism.
1944–89	The Cold War.
1947–75	End of great colonial empires; many new Third World states.
1960s	Civil Rights movement in the USA; black people enfranchised.
1968	Civil Rights movement in Northern Ireland begins decades of violence.
1979	Islamic Fundamentalists take power in Iran.
1988–94	Massacres in Burundi and Rwanda.
1989–91	Overthrow of communism in Eastern Europe and the USSR.
1989	Tiananmen Square protests in China.
1990	Britain: demonstrations against the Poll Tax force its withdrawal. Myanmar (Burma): National League for Democracy wins elections but is prevented from taking power.
1992	India: Ayodhya mosque destroyed. Italy: Proportional Representation largely abandoned.
1992–96	Civil War in Bosnia.
1998	Liberalizing president, Khatami, elected in Iran.
1998–99	Rebellion and western intervention in Kosovo.
1999	Devolved parliaments set up in Scotland and Wales. Resignation of the European Commission.
2000	Many popular protests, including destruction of genetically modified crops in Britain, action by road hauliers in several countries, and mass demonstrations against the World Trade Organization in Prague. Danish referendum rejects membership of the European monetary system.

Glossary

absolutism
monarchical government with virtually
unchallenged authority.

accountable
held answerable for decisions and actions.

amendment
alteration, made at a later date to an existing
document such as a constitution.

aristocracy
government by a noble elite; also describes the
nobility itself.

autocracy
rule by one individual with unlimited
authority.

ballot
vote. Voting slips are placed in ballot boxes.

cabinet
body consisting of the most important
government ministers.

coalition
alliance of political parties to form a
government.

command economy
economy in which all production, pricings etc.
are controlled by a central authority.

constitution
fundamental laws of a state, usually in the form
of one or more documents.

despot
ruler with absolute power based on force.

devolution
transfer of a certain amount of authority from
central to regional governments.

direct democracy
the entire people making day-to-day decisions.

ethnic
describes a group with a distinctive character,
based on features such as language, skin colour
or religion.

executive
individual or body that carries out the laws; the
government.

federation
a state created by a union of provinces or states
which grant only limited powers to the central
or federal government.

franchise
the right to vote.

Freedom of Information Act
legislation giving citizens right of access to state
documents.

globalization
situation where economic forces are
international in scale, affecting nations in ways
their governments find hard to control.

judiciary
the judges and the legal system as a branch of
government.

legislature
the law-making assembly or assemblies.

Left, left-wing
associated with socialism or communism.

literacy test
test of reading ability; where it exists, those who
fail it cannot vote.

media
newspapers, radio, TV and other forms of mass
communication.

multi-party
with several or many parties.

Resources

oligarchy
government by the few. The term is used to show disapproval.

popular sovereignty
the idea that the people is the true ruler.

racist
hostile to people who belong to a different ethnic group.

radical
describes policies or beliefs that aim to achieve fundamental changes.

representative democracy
democracy in which people choose governments and law-makers to represent them.

Right, right-wing
associated with conservative or traditional attitudes.

suffrage
the right to vote.

suffragette
in Britain, a militant woman agitator for the vote.

unitary state
one in which the central government has full authority, unlike the central government in a federation.

TV viewers can see what is going on in legislatures from day to day, and there are frequent debates and programmes about issues. Visits to legislatures and local government institutions are also easy to arrange. It is worth experiencing real politics, since novels and films, however good, tend to concentrate on exceptional, highly dramatic or comic situations. But as long as this is remembered, they can be informative as well as entertaining.

Novels
Rex Warner's *Pericles the Athenian* (1963) describes the career of the ancient Greek democratic leader, telling a good story while staying close to the known facts.
Benjamin Disraeli's *Sybil, or the Two Nations* (1845) and George Eliot's *Felix Holt, the Radical* (1866) evoke 19th-century British politics.
Robert Penn Warren's *All the King's Men* (1946) chronicles the rise and fall of a ruthless popular leader in the USA, based on the career of a real politician.

Films
One of the few films showing a lengthy debate is *Twelve Angry Men* (1957), about a jury trying to reach a verdict.
A gripping film was made of the book *All the King's Men* (1950).
In *All the President's Men* (1976) two journalists attempt to unravel the Watergate affair. (The 'Men' in all three titles is an interesting coincidence!)
Bob Roberts (1992) charts the career of a crooked politician who deceives the US public and becomes a popular hero.

Index

Africa 47-48, 51, 52
Althing 18
American Revolution 25-28
aristocracy 11, 16
Aristotle 13, 14
Asia 40, 47-48
Athens 10, 11-14

ballot, secret 5, 34
Bentham, Jeremy 35

China 9, 44, 52, 54
citizens 4, 5, 9
Cold War 44-46, 47
Commons, House of 21, 23, 35, 36
communism 41, 42, 44, 45, 46, 50, 51
Congress (US) 28
conservative 33
constitution 7, 8, 15, 16, 33, 47, 57
    American 24, 27, 28, 38, 49
    French 29, 30
    Soviet 44
corruption 46, 47, 48, 54, 59
Cromwell, Oliver 22, 23

Declaration of Independence 25, 26, 27
democracy
    direct 5, 11
    liberal 33
    representative 5
devolution 58
dictators 17, 22, 30, 43, 45, 48, 51, 57
direct action 58

elections 5, 6, 54, 55
ethnic conflicts 52-53
executive 7, 24, 28

fascism 43, 44, 45
federations 27, 34, 36
feudal system 19

France 34, 39, 55
franchise 32, 34
freedom 4, 8
French Revolution 29-30, 31, 33

Germany 34, 39, 40, 43, 47, 55
gerrymandering 49
globalization 59
government, branches of 7, 24, 28 (see also legislature)
Greeks, ancient 4, 10-14, 16

Hitler, Adolf 43, 44, 45

India 39, 48, 52-53
Industrial Revolution 31, 41
Ireland 49, 53
Islamic Fundamentalism 51

Jackson, Andrew 32
Jefferson, Thomas 25, 27
judiciary 7, 24, 28

King, Martin Luther 49, 50

laws 5, 7, 8, 9, 10, 19, 22, 28
    Rule of Law 10, 24
legislature 7, 8, 24, 28, 36, 54, 55, 56
Lenin 42
Levellers 23
liberal 33
Lincoln, Abraham 4
Lords, House of 21, 23, 36

Magna Carta 20
Marx, Karl 41, 42
media 56-57
monarchs 9, 10, 18, 19, 20, 23, 29, 33, 35, 51, 54
Montesquieu 24

oligarchy 11, 16
parliaments 18, 20

English/British 21-23, 25, 27, 36
parties, political 5, 6, 7, 23, 40, 41, 42, 43, 47, 54, 55, 56
Pericles 12
Plato 13, 14
popular sovereignty 4
presidents 28, 43
pressure groups 55
prime ministers 28, 35, 43
Proportional Representation 54, 55

referendums 57
Reichstag 34
republic 15, 16, 22, 28
Romans, ancient 15-17, 18
Russia 34, 39, 42, 44, 50, 52
    (see also Soviet Union)

Separation of Powers 24, 28
slavery 13, 27, 32, 38, 49, 50
socialism 40, 41, 42
South Africa 51
Soviet Union 42, 44, 45, 50
suffrage 30, 34, 37, 51
    women's 37-39, 40
Suu Kyi, Aung San 52

Three Estates 19, 20, 29

USA 4, 6, 8, 25-28, 32, 33, 34, 36, 37, 38, 39, 54, 55
Utilitarianism 35

voting 5, 6, 7-8, 11, 30, 34, 49, 57, 58 (see also ballot, franchise, suffrage)

Washington, George 25, 26, 28
Watergate 57, 63
Wilson, Woodrow 40

Yugoslavia 53